LANCASHIRE COUNTY LIBRARY

D0682390

My First Book of London

Charlotte Guillain • Illustrated by Roland Dry

BLOOMSBURY

LONDON OXFORD NEW YORK NEW DELHI SYDNEY

Lancashire Library Services	
30118137184747	
PETERS	J914.21GUI
£6.99	29-Nov-2018
NHA	

Bloomsbury Children's Books
An imprint of Bloomsbury Publishing Plc

50 Bedford Square
London
WC1B 3DP
UK

www.bloomsbury.com

BLOOMSBURY and the Diana logo are trademarks of Bloomsbury Publishing Plc

Copyright © Bloomsbury Children's Books, 2018
Illustrations copyright © Roland Dry, 2018
Text copyright © Charlotte Guillain

Charlotte Gullain and Roland Dry have asserted their rights under the Copyright,
Designs and Patents Act, 1988, to be identified as Author and Illustrator of this work.

All rights reserved. No part of this publication may be reproduced or transmitted in any form or by any means,
electronic or mechanical, including photocopying, recording, or any information storage or retrieval system,
without prior permission in writing from the publishers.

A catalogue record for this book is available from the British Library.

ISBN 978 1 4088 9760 7

Printed and bound in China by Leo Paper Products, Heshan, Guangdong

This book is produced using paper that is made from wood grown in managed, sustainable forests.
It is natural, renewable and recyclable. The logging and manufacturing processes conform to the
environmental regulations of the country of origin.

To find out more about our authors and books visit www.bloomsbury.com. Here you will find extracts,
author interviews, details of forthcoming events and the option to sign up for our newsletters.

Contents

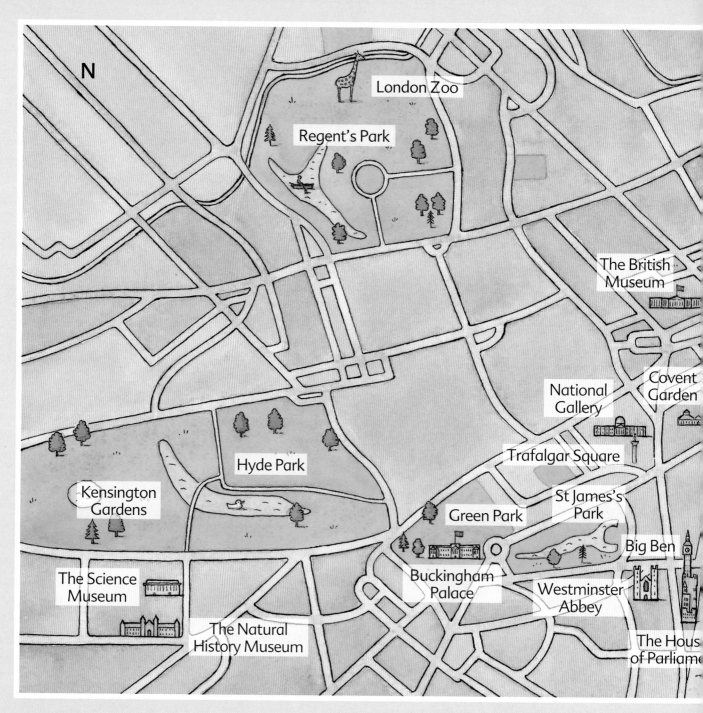

N

London Zoo

Regent's Park

The British Museum

National Gallery

Covent Garden

Trafalgar Square

Hyde Park

Kensington Gardens

St James's Park

Green Park

Big Ben

The Science Museum

Buckingham Palace

Westminster Abbey

The Natural History Museum

The House of Parliame

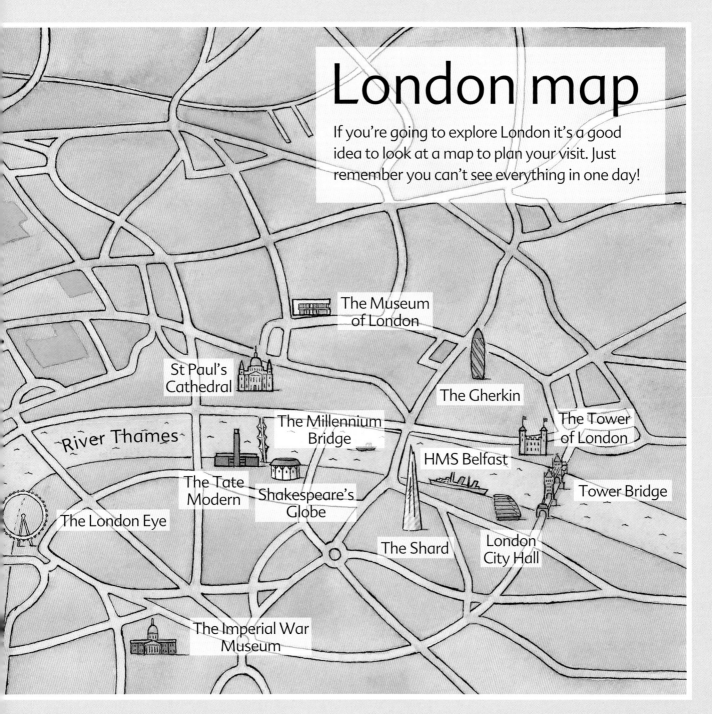

London map

If you're going to explore London it's a good idea to look at a map to plan your visit. Just remember you can't see everything in one day!

The Museum of London

St Paul's Cathedral

The Gherkin

The Millennium Bridge

The Tower of London

River Thames

HMS Belfast

The Tate Modern

Shakespeare's Globe

Tower Bridge

The London Eye

The Shard

London City Hall

The Imperial War Museum

Special things to spot

London is an exciting city to visit. There are so many interesting buildings and places to look at and discover. As you travel around there are lots of smaller things to look out for too! Many are special things that you will only find in London. While you're exploring the city, see if you can spot any of these:

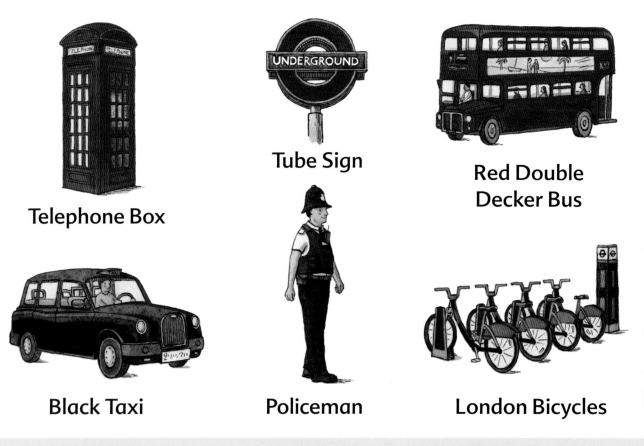

Telephone Box

Tube Sign

Red Double Decker Bus

Black Taxi

Policeman

London Bicycles

I can see a very big building behind some high railings. A flag is flying on the roof. A group of guards in red uniforms and tall black hats is marching in front of the building.

Where am I?

I am at Buckingham Palace!

This huge building is the Queen's home. Every morning during the summer you can watch the Changing of the Guard. This is when the soldiers in the red uniforms and bearskin hats march in front of the palace and swap places.

There's always a flag flying at Buckingham Palace. The Union flag that you can see in the picture flies when the Queen is not there. The Royal Standard flies when the Queen is at home.

What to look out for...

If you visit Buckingham Palace, look for these sights. You can only see some of these special things at certain times or on important days.

The Royal Standard Flag

The Changing of the Guard

The Balcony

The Gold State Coach

A Horse Guard

The Victoria Memorial

I am in a large hall with a high ceiling. There's a big staircase with a huge section of tree trunk on it. I'm looking up at an enormous whale skeleton with a gigantic mouth and a long tail.

Where am I?

I am at the Natural History Museum!

This museum is full of exhibits from the natural world. The entrance is home to a life-sized model of a blue whale suspended in the air. There's a gallery packed with dinosaur skeletons and models.

You could explore the world of creepy crawlies or find out what it's like to be in an earthquake. Visit Cocoon to find out how scientists work with the natural world today.

What to look out for...

If you go to the Natural History Museum, there's too much to see in one visit. Here are some exciting things you could look out for:

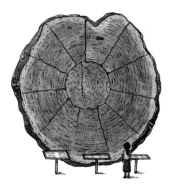

The Giant Sequoia

The Colossal Squid

The Creepy Crawlies Gallery

The Animatronic *Tyrannosaurus Rex*

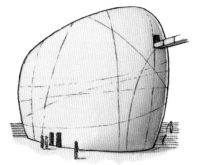

Cocoon

I can see someone on top of a very tall pillar. He's looking down at a big square. There are four bronze lions and fountains in the square, and four other statues.

Where am I?

I am in Trafalgar Square!

This busy square is 200 years old. Nelson's Column is in the middle, with a statue of Admiral Nelson on top. The square is named after the Battle of Trafalgar where Nelson beat the French leader, Napoleon.

The National Gallery is on one side of the square. At Christmas you can see a huge Christmas tree, sent by the people of Norway.

What to look out for...

If you visit Trafalgar Square, see if you can spot these famous sights. You could also look for the Fourth Plinth, which has a different work of art on it every couple of years.

A Bronze Lion

The Fountains

Nelson's Column

St Martin-in-the-Fields

George IV Statue

I am high above the city looking down on the River Thames. I am inside a glass capsule. As it moves round I can see Big Ben and the Houses of Parliament.

Where am I?

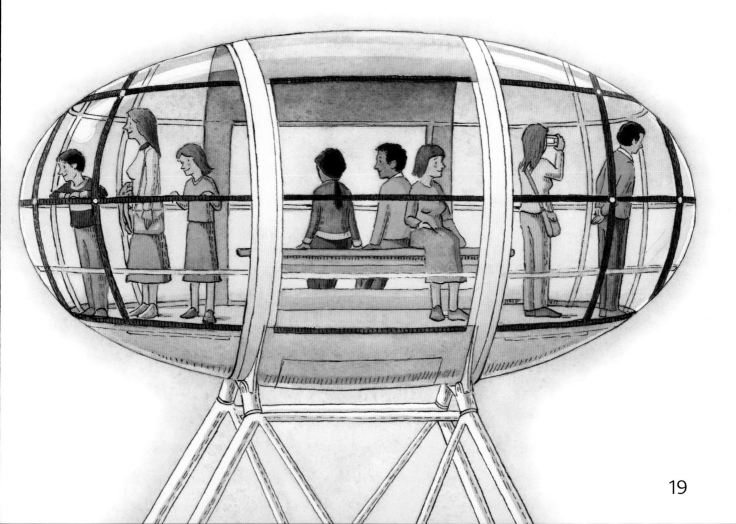

I am on the London Eye!

This big wheel by the River Thames was built in 1999 and is 135 metres high. There are 32 capsules for passengers to stand in and look out over the city. On a clear day you can see as far as 40 kilometres.

From the London Eye you can see all the bridges and boats on the river. You can also see many different types of buildings, from very old to brand new.

What to look out for...

If you go for a ride on the London Eye you will have great views across all of London. Here are some famous sights you might spot:

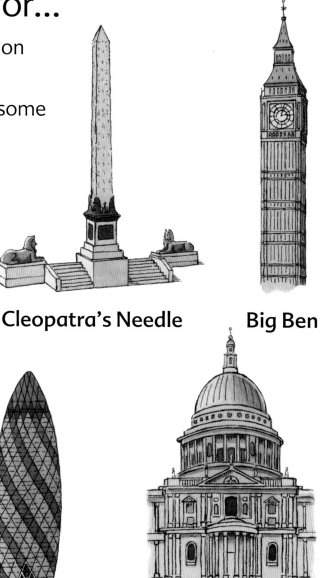

Cleopatra's Needle

Big Ben

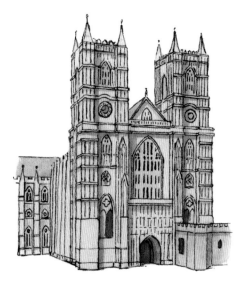

Westminster Abbey

The Gherkin

St Paul's Cathedral

I am looking at a very old building by the river. It has high walls and there are guards in special uniforms. There's a gate in the outside wall that leads into the river.

Where am I?

I am at the Tower of London!

Kings and queens lived in this fort before it was used as a prison. Prisoners came by boat along the river to Traitor's Gate in the outside wall. Many were executed on Tower Green. The Crown Jewels are still kept in the Tower today.

The guards at the Tower are called Yeoman Warders or Beefeaters. One Warder looks after the ravens at the Tower. Stories say the Tower will fall down if the ravens ever leave!

ENTRY TO THE TRAITORS GATE

What to look out for...

As you explore the inside and outside of the Tower of London, look out for these famous sights:

The Crown Jewels

HMS Belfast

A Yeoman Warder

The Traitor's Gate

Tower Bridge

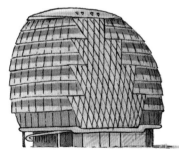

London City Hall

I am in a large courtyard with an amazing glass ceiling. In the middle of the courtyard is a round room full of books. Through a doorway there are lots of statues and carvings from Ancient Egypt.

Where am I?

I am inside the British Museum!

This is the oldest museum in the world with collections from many countries. In the Ancient Egyptian gallery there are mummies and statues of pharaohs. Other collections include weapons, armour, carvings and everyday objects from thousands of years ago.

The Great Court in the museum is the largest covered square in London. The Reading Room in its centre is home to many important books and manuscripts.

What to look out for...

There are more than six million things to see at the British Museum! Here are some interesting things to look out for when you visit:

The Reading Room

The Younger Memnon

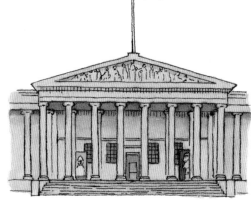

Carvings and Columns at the Entrance

Rosetta Stone

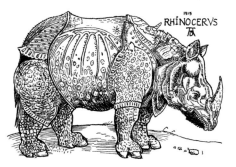

Dürer's Rhinoceros

Sutton Hoo Helmet

I am inside a big park. I can hear birds calling and animals making strange noises. Suddenly a gorilla climbs down from a tree trunk and stares at me.

Where am I?

31

I am at London Zoo!

This popular zoo is in Regent's Park and is home to over 750 types of animals and birds.

Animal Adventure is the part of the zoo where you can discover what life is like for many different animals. The Snowdon Aviary is full of birds from all over the world.

32

In the amphitheatre you can see
special Animals in Action displays.
And don't forget to visit all the creepy
crawlies in the B.U.G.S. exhibition!

What to look out for...

There are too many creatures to see at London Zoo in one visit. As you explore the zoo, look out for these amazing animals and birds:

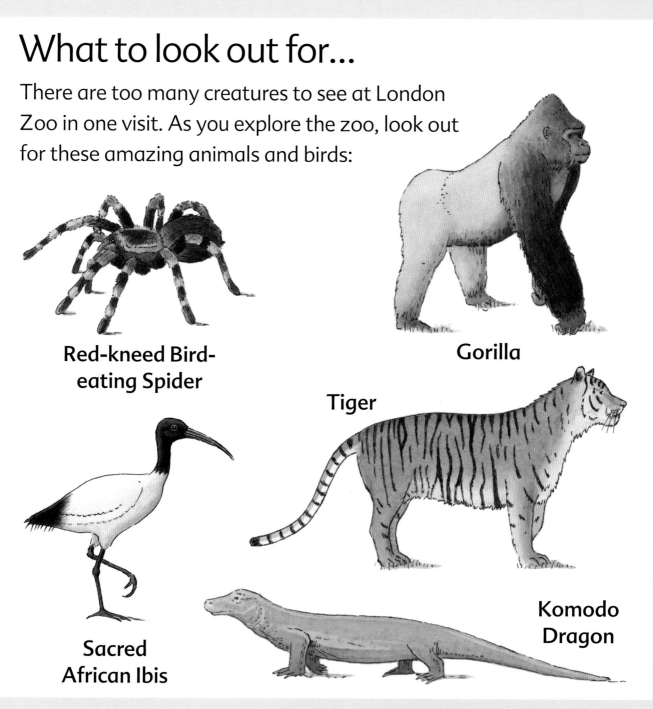

Red-kneed Bird-eating Spider

Gorilla

Tiger

Sacred African Ibis

Komodo Dragon

I am standing in a large square. There's a big hall full of shops and cafés in the middle of the square. In front of the hall there are colourful street performers entertaining a crowd.

Where am I?

35

I am in Covent Garden!

The square is called the Piazza. There used to be a market in the hall in the middle. Jugglers, musicians and other street entertainers can be seen all around the Piazza.

Just off the north side of the square is the Royal Opera House. St Paul's Church is at the other end of the Piazza. Its churchyard is a quiet place to relax in this busy part of the city.

What to look out for...

You will see something different every time you visit Covent Garden, but here are some things you can always spot:

St Paul's Church

Buskers

The Central Market

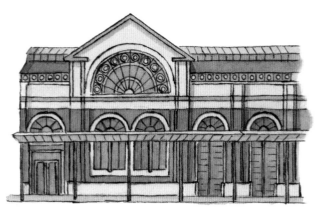

The London Transport Museum

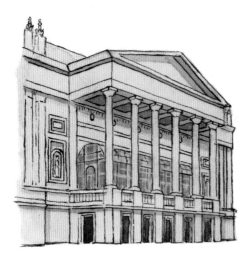

The Royal Opera House

I am looking at a very old steam engine. All around me there are inventions from history. I am in a very big building where lots of people are exploring the exciting hands-on exhibitions.

Where am I?

I am at the Science Museum!

There are seven floors with many different galleries to explore. On the ground floor you can interact with the Pattern Pod, copying and making your own patterns. Down in the basement is the Garden Gallery, where young visitors can play with water, light and sound.

On the third floor you can discover the Launchpad, which is full of interactive exhibits. There are games to play and experiments to try.

What to look out for...

You could explore the Science Museum many times and still not see everything! If you visit the museum, here are some things to look out for:

Apollo 10 Command Module

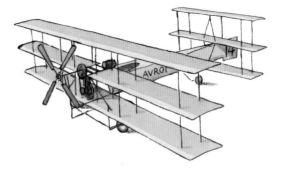

The Garden Gallery

The Launchpad

A V Roe's Triplane

I am standing inside a huge church.
I am looking up at the inside of a large
dome. People are climbing up the stairs on
the inside of the dome and looking down.
A loud, deep bell is ringing.

Where am I?

I am in St Paul's Cathedral!

This huge church was built 32 years after a spark from Farryner's bakery caused the Great Fire of London. It was designed by Sir Christopher Wren.

The cathedral's dome is one of the largest in the world. It is 111 metres high. Inside the dome is the Whispering Gallery. If someone whispers on one side of the Gallery you can hear it on the other side. The bell is called Great Paul and it strikes every day at one o'clock.

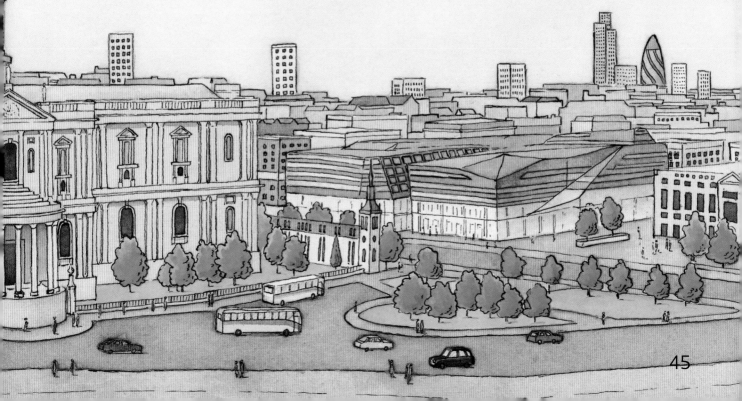

What to look out for...

When you visit St Paul's here are some famous sights to look out for inside and outside the cathedral:

The Whispering Gallery

Henry Moore's Statue

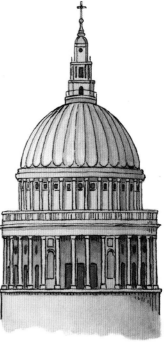

The Dome

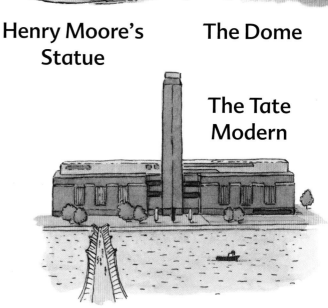

The Tate Modern

The Millennium Bridge

London words

cathedral   large important church

column   upright support on a building,
usually made of stone or brick

dome   roof shaped like half a sphere

execute   put to death

exhibit   object on display in a museum

gallery   room where art or museum objects
are shown

memorial   statue or building made to
remember a person or event

museum   building where interesting objects
are shown

opera   play that is set to music

palace   large building that is home to a
king or queen

Find out more

If you have enjoyed this book and would like to find out more about exploring London you could visit www.visitlondon.com. This website has a list of the best museums in the city for children as well as information about London events.

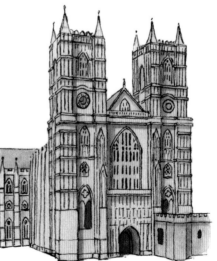

London quiz

Now you have read the book, can you answer these questions about London?

1. When does the Union flag fly on Buckingham Palace?

2. Where would you find a life-sized model of a blue whale?

3. How old is Trafalgar Square?

4. How high is the London Eye?

5. What are the guards at the Tower of London called?

6. Which museum is the oldest in the world?

7. How many types of animals and birds are there in London zoo?

8. Where in London might you see buskers?

9. Where can you copy and make your own patterns?

10. How high is the dome in St Paul's Cathedral?